Restorations

In memory of my parents, Joyce and Peter Hudis

Restorations

Rosalind Hudis

Seren is the book imprint of
Poetry Wales Press Ltd.
Suite 6, 4 Derwen Road, Bridgend, Wales, CF31 1LH
www.serenbooks.com
facebook.com/SerenBooks
twitter@SerenBooks

The right of Rosalind Hudis to be identified as
the author of this work has been asserted in accordance
with the Copyright, Designs and Patents Act, 1988.

ISBN: 978-1-78172-608-2
ebook: 978-1-78172-609-9

A CIP record for this title is available from the British Library.

The publisher acknowledges the financial assistance of the Books Council of Wales.

Cover artwork: Ffos-y-Ffin
(16.5 x 17 inches acrylic on paper 2019)
www.elfynlewis.com

Author photograph: Hayley Madden for the Poetry Society.

Printed in Bembo by Severn, Gloucester.

Contents

Shellac

It has archived anaemia: *The Philips London Library globe*
lowered
onto kit-box shelves in my parents' front-room.

Blue faded from an imperial lush,
continents as techni-thin green or lemon
like magic painting
a collusion with flattened zones
for military convenience.

The world is traversable in Latinate script
variably sized with a hidden reasoning
why Tashkent is larger than Alaska.
It creaks on turning   dense

longitude and tribes,
impossibly fragile.

Told 'not a toy' we sense how all that sediment,
time,
expansion
all the geography hours inflicted by dad
rest on two demi-hemispheres of paper
glued
pre-digital, childhood's dissolvable work.
Origami shadows, balsa-wood spit-fires, paper
shaped,
torn,
spilt on,
limp.

A globe's constructed like a face:
epidermis pasted to a mould
plastered,
papered. Inside a wooden cross
pinned to the equator. It carries losses,
a thickened, darkened surface.

Panelled in
under a weight of old shellac and later, wax
mouse-trailed with gunk,
six thousand stars and planets on the Celestial Globe,
the original so thin, belief
is all that reels them out across space and cobalt.

Fitzroy's Barometer

We almost miss it, exchanging tableau chaiselongues
for wasps and cream in the castle cafeteria.
We weren't shown to its corner spot
holding on to atmosphere, musty frame
where morales rise and fall

with weather's life-cycle.
Haven't we always been hooked
on fluctuation? – even the deer –
(rippled here among birches)
whose snuffles make a chart of us

as time does. Think of Fitzroy
in the man-shed of his cabin: squints to read,
logs measurement through the slow curve it takes
to furl 'f's, square light to moisture,
outside buttressed

against the weight of in. As I tweet
this, response flicks back, no slow
erosions: a siphon tube sunk
in old snow of aged paper, mercury crusted
to a dirty ice-cap.

Here, sulphuric green sludge has mushed
the angle out of a hinge. Unlike Google Earth
this vista is for shrinking; inner tubes
hold a tiny rivering script
in ink like weak coffee

and Himalayas are sketched
in a wavery outline, an old man's flashback
behind numbered horizontals.
Scree flows, crevasses, whole mountain ranges squeezed
into the doll's house of eleven inches.

My lap-top pumps out a language without gaps.
I dive down, rise away, restless for the endless
flora that keeps on regenerating. But Fitzroy's barometer steadies
towards the invisible now. There are liver spots in corners;
fissures in the paper raise the moon.

Fixative

The cormorant holding out his wings
and your eyes holding out with him.

A barometer's dial, in-between spaces, patch
sewn to a baby's heart, stuff that congeals atoms.

Formaldehyde, salt on anything, coat of ashes
stair-rungs to aircraft, syntax, ozone, pollen.

Gum, spikes, lime-wash, salad cream, magnetism, stars
a metal hip, fossils in cement, the golden ratios,

weight of carbon monoxide,
how a day grips like shellfish. This photo:

us in the 1960s, playing on a bombsite
the man who dipped us in sulphate, vanishing

silver halide, silver that held us
not darkened or fogging, so that always our stares

unweather from a storm of greys, willed there
until whoever looked, looked elsewhere.

Last Sighting

Vasari's Last Supper. Florence flood 1966

Water unmarvelled us
dissolved tone, loaves, left
a milky indecision,
like the start of blindness.

Black seeped
round the borders, shrank
our perspective
to a pinhole.

Our wreathed arms
sagged, snagged the circuit
of lines leaping
from robe to robe.

Yellows, blue, carmine
rewilded; we slurred
in a moth fog, lost
difference.

A pink smear remained
on Judas, a sweetener
— the departing
drag of sunset. His face.

Isinglass

(Leningrad 1941)

It is yellowish, translucent, smells faintly of fingers
warmed against a crotch. I soften it slowly on so little fire.
Wait. Waiting is the fourth ingredient
the slow burner in which you feed on aromas of life.
We've become very good at this.

My husband restores art at the Palace
but today he braced their windows with paper strips,
his thumbs pressing them in place, only
small joints to stave off shattering.
We hold everything together with shreds.

For restoring, you must cut the hard glue into pieces
soak in brandy in a vessel of clay or glass.
It must be covered, but leave the pan half-empty:
nothing restores without emptiness.
When the glue has softened, melt in a boiler, add garlic.

This is the gel my husband has so delicately guided
under paint; he would use a microscope
but I know the persistence of his hands. I imagine
fragments regrouping to a still-life of grapes, lobster,
umbers and velvet.

A corpse palette.
They say a meal's two parts metaphor –
for dinner we pour glue into bowls
call it brûlée, call it art.

How to Make Restorer's Glue

Locate a sturgeon from the black seas,
mammary fish that swell through shadows
eyes dull, snouts flat, but fanged for man-eating
yet browse seal pups newly swimming, whole shoals
of crayfish on a current. Haul it steaming
onto the harbour. Slit. Gentle

out the bladder – slippery
it will flop through your hands.
Slit. It's sleek with membranes, like vernix.
Strip these, expose. In the air they will dry a little;
roll them to mimic fingers.

Staple. Press each finger
to a heart shape. Dry out.

Jerome in the Desert

There is no let-up here; sky
which could pose balm
aches with its permanence.

He stands on craters,
his skin's a twist
of dried desiderata.

The Trinity
lowering over him
is hardly an epiphany

hardly the light-show
that means it's over.
Oxygen has stalled

in the hot end of the palette,
won't turn its beatitude
towards green.

The Artist Mixes Colour in the Renaissance

Don't think of me as lime-robed and lost
in undailiness; I come with sleeves rolled-up,
worker in a mire of substance. Yes, I stink!

I chew on a rotted wafer of dried fish glue
my saliva in the mix. How else to stretch the hue
of some frosty cleric? My paints are part kill:

rabbit skin, horse hoof, pig's blood.
I knife, mine, grind, churn, pound, steep, sweat
my way to that primal blue you worship.

When you varnish me with meaning, remember
the grit under my nails, the fumes. Green
comes from the labour camps you made

for your longing. And that hair-coiled girl
resolved from light. She's no touched-up
pink fix. She took on the earth

to coagulate: egg-yolk, red clay, mineral, old linen
marble dust. Do you think, if she looked up
she wouldn't roar with the energy of her roots?

Consolidant

The maker found his mannequin that night,
a back-street beauty, the raking light of a strip
bulb exposed her as layerless – just the colour
of nylons set abstractly. You could do anything with that.
He sawed off five of her fingers

set them in rucked paint on a board. They were caught
pre-actless, suggestive. Where could they go
but into anyone's skeletons? They were frisson,
butchery, celebration. Three adjectives up
from plastic, made them art.

We found her another night: she was leaving
herself behind in flakes, paint scratchings
(her, as in body part). All grime, rebellion.
Made herself at home in soft entropy
the joy of not giving a dime about her substrate.

We're restorers, paid to re-set that fixture
you bought. We turned the infra-red on her
exposed her particles, saw her sticky traces,
a past life of beeswax in her crevices. Decided
to impregnate. We'd re-bond her to the dream

she hatched from. We levelled the ultrasonic mister,
held her under until the stink and fog were over.
She was slippery with sturgeon glue. We hadn't done.
For hours we pressed her flakes back with spatulas.
By daylight she was bland. You pay a lot for that.

Mère Poussepin

portrait by Gwen John

I don't have you alive, just this flat memory sketched
in black and white, two centuries old. My brief to bring you
back into vivid dimension, a holy now. The nuns want you
in each room, like heating. Thirteen yous, your eyes
everywhere, Foundress, foundry. I am known for versions.

Unlike Galatea, you won't rise biddable and milky
from hard matter. I will put the hard matter back into
your peaceable hand arrangement. Iron. Complexity.
Huge hands, they won't stay folded in a feminine ending,
their energy a concertina. That's the gesture before a laugh

large enough to shake the steeple. And look at the mannish lean
forward of your shoulder, a shrug, a challenge, not angled to submit.
Your habit will be granite cliff-face, not penitence in some drab
variant on scratchy. You will gaze at us full-frontal, wry-lipped,
your smile is irony, will send: you called me. Here I quip.

Inherent Vice

When the painting arrived on a stretcher, restorers
who'd rushed it for x-ray
found its make-up pungent with traces
over oil paint, the artist had spilt
grease
liquid rubber, his own urine,
ash.
His famous desert colour was by-product
waste, layered toxins. His 'monumental vista'
of twinned towers were shadowy
strips, stapled to the surface
like bills.
All were torn. Some tacked back, askew.

The foam was breaking
down, grease softening, smudging, a cataract
over his 'clarity of purpose'. It caught dust, the last
black powders of a blue-bottle, minute silage
of dead people or traffic going anywhere
but a gallery. Hairs.

They improvised for now, a patch-up
lesser than the blue-print, glued shreds back, for hours
picked dirt with tweezers. They squinted
over smudged tracks where tear might
hook to tear.

For soft rubber
they could do nothing. After twenty-five years
cells crumble, footholds vanish. Like a pitted
hard drive, surface meanings
rubbed out by being simply
under the sun.

Portrait of the Artist as a Pear

She has chosen to escape through a fruit.
It's not a door. Doors slice into the space
she stands in; she'd fall through the cut
take the ache of a change of key
with her like involuntary rudeness.

This way she's there,
yet leaves and her leaving seems
partitioned but part of the texture
of where she continues to stand,
blue bowl, red olives

moony garlic

the conditional yellows of a pear

although every stroke she adds
to ripen the skin, dissolves her.

Millais Floats Ophelia

soluble across brown

        that's never one thing sucks in
        everything it moistens

                        feeds, in-

        fuses even the hurts returned
        as apricot crow flowers apple

        green nettles

                through a twisted willow

        loosestrife poppy primrose
                on water denser
                    than earth
                    their pigments brim
                          generous as yolk

            her epitaph:

            there's nothing less immobile
              than her corpse leaching
              its corollaries into the river

              a voyeur's corruption
            of whatever   resistance
            might once have glued her —
                  obstinate
              stray intelligence

                never floral

           Cue in The Body Snatchers, the sirens
                of soft focus
                  in pace

File By

Glass patrols the border between them: Him
waxy souvenir of the face that sprouted
fungal on towers, hovered
over every exit, intimate
as the butcher next door now, but insulated
from sweat or cheap cologne veiling the runnel
of fear that's routine as a hormone, oils
each cog of this hour

where they are led by like children or animals
who have to see to believe the death
who are briefly permitted a peep-show/warning
(see – he is *ever-fresh*)
but might dare how much formaldehyde,
powder, tweaking
hides carnage, or how mildly debased
his pose, by frilled white pillows

and might clench against the urge
to piss, or giggle or gossip
in whispers about that liver spot, tufted
mole; one more passage
like so many, sedimented shuffling,
queues that box in a day,
is unlike: the first side-stepping
hope, being the ones who walk out.

How to Tenderize a Word

Take a word like *torture* – wherever you buy it –
it's tough, won't chew down without the aid
of classy practices. Its shocked cells locked
rigid at the point of butchery, stay locked
in the swift passage to freezer. No time, no grace,
to loosen. And show me the butcher
who will let words hang
in forgiving back passages, their syllables
softly dislocating. Come in the marinade!

Lie your word face up in a metal container.
Slowly submerge in a mixture of sweet and acid.
Vinegar will do, pineapple if you wish
for a dash of the Caribbean. But any flavour
you choose will serve to suffuse
with overlays of atmosphere, make tender,
exude a confession of bikinied heat
of Moroccan palaces or Mexican stars.
Flesh will be there somewhere – a hinted pheromone

so close to fear – teasing, a spice, an electric trace.

Theory of Stradivarian Sound

In the end it was a matter of woodworm:
decay-drunk hoppers
from the forest to interiors where sitting
was now an art-form on props.

Fine-tuned tables, instruments
were pocked and tunnelled in oil paint
Italian air. But the fable needs exceptions
nicely supplied at Cremona

where violins stayed unchewed-perfect.
Stradivari sound could be pinned
on insecticide: a coating of chromium
fluoride, borax.

Chemicals for the next life, their crystals
mixed, like an afterthought of snow
into the hollowed body, cloaking
the dried-out heart.

Natural Hazards

Already water has entered the house
soaked the four corners of its timeline
shivered them like a mirage on an empty road.
I should have followed advice – kept out
'hazards to historic artefacts'.

Too much light has paled the quilts
drained them of vinegary deodorants;
there is nothing here to say we hid
behind a varnish of evocative air.
The body and its hope have gone,

our hormones a brief commercial.
What was given and taken are tribal
maps of fungi, or at a certain angle
a planet rising green from the lens
of the Hubble, not yet annealed.

Interior

The house they rent is wholly *magnolia*.
They can change, if they wish, to *linen*.
Tranquil's in the contract, so no, their daughters
may not paint this room black.

It mottles anyway, exposes a puce blur
the shape of a kidney, where one sister
drew in jam the fate of another.
These chalked anthropoids are the family

each member with a coin head
coin belly: you'd know the mother
because she's fattest. Here is the blur
of a lobbed plate, archaeology of chocolate,

faint fly carnage and the scars
of top skin torn from walls
with letters no longer wanted: interview,
love-tryst, heart scan.

Here is the underworld: intricate
mud Pollocks mushed by the soft
dissolution of moths, and here scores, deep
in plaster, marking where someone left.

Gallery

What unfolds, on my loose meander, is the scale of crumpling.
Here and there, a crumple-free jerkin, reformation black, strictly
without exuberant reference. But mostly it's crush or flounce,
a whole life-story in creases, and it seems, more folds in drape
equals closer to God, or at least a place on the plateau
above lowlife. Weightiness gathers towards the point
of attention: a toffee-smooth infant Christ, whose one first crease,
in the tummy zone, bodes freight-loads to come.

Saints and clerics have mastered the time past of their folds
into an eternal now, wear them like classic cuts,
deserving their pure blues. What would they have said
about the glorious slippage into body-fest? Titian's mass crumples
of silk adoring itself and the belly-fat rippling beyond it.
Or Rembrandt's focus on face, all centred on the nose
that's replaced the little Christ, and greying fluffles
of hair that were once attendant cloud puffs.

Next room, the down-grade's complete; an apron sags
half-mindedly from the hips of a woman in a doorway.
In front, her husband on pit-strike, his trousers miscreased
at the knees. Both look inwards and sideways, distracted,
anywhere but towards sun that's flooded their aborted morning.
No day's shape to step into. No Saturday difference
when she might soak shirts, iron furiously for the Sabbath,
erasing the grimed-in way cloth takes their fatigue.

Book of Masters

Dad believes in Art, lowers his holy book
like an injured moth, a transient thing
that could crumble or vanish

but smells Biblic: behind tissue, pictures
glued on, and sometimes lifting
at edges, the pink ripple wings

in the fresco he uncovers. We skim
the cross-eyed stare of angels
their melt-away skin. Beyond

lemon groves and towers,
fleshy murder in forests, gods
change someone to hairy

or branching, behind varnish.
Paris swells from dots,
a dancer curls in chalk motion

to fix a shoe, splodge crows swerve
down a fast-track sky. I pause
at *The Conversation*: a standing man

in striped pyjamas, who won't sit down,
a seated woman in black who will not stand.
And what they said they've said dad says

or not yet spoken – neither can leave
the flat blue that gums them
to this moment. The space between

is a painting, or a window on the garden,
poplar tree, pond, path, sky, lawn, shadow them.
Within that view a duplicate tiny version.

I crane in, find my grandmother bending
to break blue poppy heads,
grandfather stilled and rigid in a window.

It's hot, bees whine, a haze striated
like wings. He stays behind glass
she, silent, goes on breaking.

Paris

Lime trees are dumb with chlorophyll
wasps nurse whatever sweetness
the makers of crepe and *beignets*
have smeared on the glistening air.

They hang like half-cut bodyguards
above the bent back of a girl
who's thumbing the racks of vinyl.

She sifts with forensic tip-fingers
an archaeologist hunting codes
locked in shimmer. Scratches buzz
gyrate a counter-line, off-
beat, off-their heads, swamp crazy

jazz, quivering on the city's white pate.

Or With Open Window

A Corner of the Artist's Studio in Paris by Gwen John

If she could agree to be this room
or the other. Possibility pleats her.

Not *there,* her outline sealed,
but spreading, invisible, in two takes:

One corner, one window, netted
unnetted, above a table

that's the still crossfire
where her looking springs out

from an open book or coils back
into a crease of wired flowers.

On a white chair her blue coat streams
labile, could let her slide

through each frame. Even this one
where the window is closed,

hard edges inside
a stockade of angles.

Or *with Open Window*:
the room's misted; sharp

in the distance, she's hung a tent
of reflections and sky.

Where she waits can be folded/
unfolded like her paused umbrella,

like triangled sunlight on the wall
that could pin her to its moment

or, warming outwards, paint her
into the visible.

The Angels Consider Their Restoration

It's dark in this sphere of heaven.
Wasn't it always?
We have been here a long time
our voices precede and follow us
when you look at us you imagine
a whitewash of song.

We have lost colour
what was peachy
has rusted and cracked –
flesh mossed over
but our lips are clear.

We too imagine song.

We look at the shapes of sound
in our minds
paint bubbling to a rhythm.

New skin
raw babyish
under the crusted scar

we see you craning
your insect scrutiny
no bigger than a semi-breve

canvas
for an old idea.

Over and over
the same song oblivious
that sound decays.

Lasers can lift layers,
scum, dead crust,
back to the garden.

It is dark in this sphere of heaven
and that carries on
no pink under-myth –

you think we're a garden?
Celestial paeans
budding
on those brand Renaissance lips?

Get us out of here!

We are adipose with time
our descendants
still hooked to the itchy

armature of goose wings
brinked on concrete
above the usual metropolis.

Before the paint dries
seals us in rose botox

let us come clean
trailing rot
in all its bruise-blue glory

let us re-scale your synapses
to the event horizon

there was never
an option to reverse.

Hospital Art

My father's on the third floor, signed in blue
for cardiac. Red's respiratory
green is bowels.
It's a simple code to take the pain
out of nuance. But down this corridor
I play the curvature of blues:
mauve dolphins
in a primary sea,
a peeling shell-blue Vishnu
on a billboard in Bombay,
blue-lit saxophones,
an illicit behind-doors-blue
blue winking
like a timed prescription.

And now blue gloves to view
a body, wintered in this holding space.
Memory is porous. I conjure creosote
stinging the marshes, a man who scrapes
blue flakes from his dinghy's hull,
swears when salt burns a cut.
His eyes are bland,
nothing to light on but the ripple of digits.
I could start there, pour in flint shingle,
mudflats, jetty, one cloudy heron
bending to prick the surface,
a blue skiff that dissolves
in a rain-shaft on the skyline,
reappears.

Minutiae

Emptying this last room, I catch myself at the spot
where my father watched the garden lose its grip
as he did. Outside, the greenhouse grimed
with old breath, a place of husks, blurred webs,

the stink of geraniums past. Labels remain,
obsessively cursive, their season blotted over.
But still, in packets, a smattering of seeds
holed up in themselves and scentless

which changes the view; less skeleton
than something latent – unfulfilled borders
except in his inner mind where schemes
of yellow and rose out-shone the loss.

If I conjure him, it's not a white pandemic
of endings, but the detail of micro life:
he's in the vaults of a seedbank, opens
stacked drawers where bag nestles on bag

labelled. He reaches to feel each one,
how each husk names itself,
muscular, fretted, black
phosphoric, ferrous, grey, rose

creped or smooth, uterine, fractal,
whorled, crumbled as cinders yet not soft.
Like children, he wants them not to break
too soon. Seed can be forced if you storm it

gnaw at fault-lines, fake an immobile daylight
lock in a room of winter, add salt or sugar
hood, let water engulf and drain or simply
narrow time. The greenhouse hordes its time

in faith, is my father bent to press a soil surface,
lining up seeds like moments, each one a shade
unlike another, living the preparation.
its length and minutiae, his dark blue ink.

Edgeland Map

impossible to handle, like a cranky pet
in our narrow car, refused to lie down in deference
to rules, played limp on opening

hitch-hiked the wind, tore along some latitude
where our campsite was stowed, the cow-pats
the mushy fringes, through which we couldn't go.

Map and friction were one. I never learned to close it,
never got the hang of self-location, saw only un-rule
on a medical green, contours as an auntish crochet

unravelling, rivers a blue varicose wiggle.
It was personal, confirmed the unfixable in me,
an unfindable road. Maps lost their edges

to mist, dark angels, bulge-cheeked cherubs
blowing in vain. I saw the finger not the ground
truthed, until now when mapless

I try to find an iris in the white
of your dementia and here the path digs down,
not across, a mind re-rooted

in snow.

Esk

uncrumples like an eyelid after sleep
                         looks back at us, opaque
then streams to gather pace, a rush of purpose
                         only to eddy down
almost to motionless.

It does elastic things to sound –
                         the spiel of water, pigeons
cuts out, our breathing
wetly close before river-talk gushes back
                         except we've missed a link
in its stop/start syntax, like the gap between
light pulses, or the way one self in a stop-frame reel
                         steps, spectral, from another.
There must be a blink of not
being as if our new physics is holed
                         with wishless wells
into which I step, remembering us by the Esk
                         before your mind slipped
and I'd watch a thought flow over your face
                         try to stretch the folds
of speech-muscle in each corner of your mouth
then cave-back, crumple-in, before I could lay hold.
Your eyes cloud like skin forming.
                         I stir you and they clear, the becoming
of one you into another is full of erasures.

They are the moments I recall the trees, banked
like a watch tower, shuttering
                         the bone-white sky off/on fitfully.

You liked the birches
                         for the way they gave light an equal trial.
And sun on bald patches of the precipice
                         its baked clay look, ironish, fissile
the random way it's pocked and moulded into drifts
of fossil faces.

You seemed happy to lie in your dark
                    brown deafness. Nothing
to strain towards, no heaving your mind up cliffs however warmed.

You snapped off the oxygen mask so savagely there was no rope back.
It left a fossil mark.
In the morgue I saw it on your neck, still raw.

Rift

It was a caesura
in the lift of cup to lips.
For a beat, her eyes died
then flickered back, puzzled,
as she slid
gravely to the floor.

All her words
flurried up in one sweep, left.

Some returned to the hospital
to scavenge syllables
the nut-shape of an 'o'.
We were keeping watch
by a too wide window
that laid her silence bare.

We were keeping watch
for a sound to root
like a chip of bone,
grow.

'o' would be enough
to restore her.

As 'o' restores in flickers

a part-crumbled city.
She dawdles in the vetch
beside a bombed-out terrace.

Nightly one streetlamp richens
its searchlight for her shadow
to meet uncertain others.

Veterans are younger, line
remembrance like crows.
Black rain in November.

Foghorns lowing from the dock;
her mother, Em, cups
and uncups an ear, undecided on hope.

★

The casual day when Em walks on
to work, war-time. Again
a house behind implodes.

Heat. Echo of her stilettos.

This time she returns: one side gone *utterly*
a bedroom that glows,
indecent, in late sun, a lace shade rocking.
One wall, two pegs, a man and womans' coats.

Below them, a suitcase

charred boards,
a precipice.

And then tinnitus like dawn:
the suitcase was full of starlings
is later what she repeats
and again, how she couldn't break

through air that held back, glassed.
For minutes she'd seemed to tip
down floors of her skull

For minutes, the birds.

Under

i

We've circled you like saints, on plastic chairs,
not homage but to stir you with names dropped
into the white well of your face.

We hunt you, who have sunk away
deeper than we can sound. No milky traces,
a flotilla in the darkness. Mother,

you are still being asked of – to incarnate,
touch up the foundation, if only a shadow
on the cave as another shadow pulls you:

the nurse sponging
not to soothe, but shine you back.
She asks for your lipstick, hairnet.

When you start to catch
the light your face will rise
to our surface, rouged

reassembling old knots
of home, pain, flesh:
a fable under glass

where we can look in on ourselves
shoaling a cold hearth.

ii

I sense the restorer's eye, probing.
Even down here, the heatless base layer, he raises
my temperature minutely. Perhaps he can smell
an undertow in the stairwell between varnishings.
Am I foxy, or something that catches the throat
like bog-myrtle? The ghost fish in a word
meaning dry land? Opaque layers above me
admit nothing blue. I stay afraid my life is stitched

to them, an anchor. But I long for water's memory.
His gentlest tool is sailcloth; if he finds me, it could fill
the chasms where I can't connect, patches
where my fabric's brittled, the tacks corroded. It won't
restore what's gone but I would live the ocean, slap
of wind. Cut my ties. But I know he won't let me
escape myself. He stares and stares into
my rumour because I'm wanted intact.

He has other tools: tweezers, dental picks,
clamps, droppers, scalpel. And the one I most fear
the tube he could snake down through every layer
push through my nose, burn my throat, hook me
alive in wordlessness, this desert.

Skin is a Glasshouse

is a glove, a decoy
a conveyor of news
from dead stars, a sifter
of microbes and whiskies
is a one-stop immigration office
for light waves and bugs
is weather chart, duvet, colourist
gives false intelligence,
ground truth.

And if skin performed like water?
Could be poured, shunted,
carry crayfish, tampons, mind-slick
away, fill sewers, gorges
take whatever shape means
swept out, funnelled in, stagnant
inclined to sculpt?

Skin flirts with water
lets it out to resemble a leaf
breathing, in
when a leafy veining is not
the surface of choice
keeps a lid on turbulence, lets
things pass in trickles,
when your mind's turned
relives itself in sea.

Segmentary

6.0pm: she is the place of her chair, faked velveteen.
The incontinence cover is paisley to convince
it is necessary as teacups are to beige
fluffy mules. These things are like empty clothes, not hers,
pre-set, her body lowered in, instructed to stay
performance art. For an hour, the urine table rises

7.0pm: when the cramp in her stomach reaches knifing, she's lifted
from this set, downed in the ambulance and strapped
there; a needle's arc, blue pulse, flash-jab
of junctions, slip-road, headlights.
She tries to say *an excruciation*, squeezing
the space out like toothpaste

8.0pm: is the table pulled from under the cloth which still hangs
there, briefly, little squares of fork and gleam
like teeth; sounds are deleted, then décor. Luminous
yellow bone below the door. Hungers slip from her
in pulses, tubes with them. She's draining
out of her blue gown, there you go as they sponge

9.0pm: as they sponge there you go out of her blue gown
in pulses, tubes with them. She's draining
yellow bone below the door. Hungers slip from her
like teeth; sounds are deleted then décor. Luminous
little square of fork and gleam there briefly
is the table pulled from under the cloth which still hangs

10.0pm: the space out like toothpaste
she tries to say *an excruciation* squeezing headlights
blue pulse, flash-jab of junctions, slip roads
there − a needle's arc, when the cramp in her stomach
reaches knifing, she's lifted from this set,
lowered into the scene

11.0pm: there, performance art. For an hour, the ice manages
          pre-set, instructed to stay fluffy mules.
          These things are like empty clothes, not hers,
          it is necessary as teacups are to beige.
          The keynote is paisley to convince
          she is the place of her chair, faked velveteen.

The Person on Display Has Been Replaced by a Replica

Who is this in the corner bed, by the huge window that offers a hotel vista, not a hospital?

The placing hopes they could raise their spine and see things that please and mean – the slope of hill that dips towards sea. Pier, castle, seagull, roofs. The placing hopes they will rise to the Victorian prom dream. Who is this who could look? The person on display, in her sea-front blue. The person on display resembles the person who flew. The person on display resembles a person who would accept the effort to let her view an edited beachscape (no dog turds, bad sex, junkies, sad old men). The person on display has come to mean that which must be placated in gentle obvious ways. The person on display is deemed to have lost her critical scepticism. The person on display is a vessel for our avoidance. Little kind things like souvenirs. The person on display is kept at a constant temperature. The person on display is calibrated by a catheter. The person on display is being unfleshed into stone.

She dies first on the left

good hand, marriage ring, lopped
from years of grip.

The side the sun falls
mornings, its unfelt heat.

We group on her right, catch the eye
that reflects us, tunes

to a name
on the light side of memory.

We grasp
as she grasps the bed rail

with her weak hand
where touch drops away.

When she dies on the right
her fingers meet.

Insulation

Each year your house staunched more
of the raw north-easterlies:

lagging, boiler, double perspex.
You taped and tampered with glitches,

the bubble like a lost calf lowing
in tunnels of copper pipe. Fathers

fixed, remembered fathers
who kept out talk of their war
behind triple-glazed eyes.

U-foam came like a fog
to muffle the dark spaces

around rooms that only wanted
the boom of progress. Still you conjured

weather
how to out-face it.

Hunched over weeklies
on tough gear, Gore-Tex, bought
new shields for old skin.

But I unwrap you youthful
in this un-glassed photo

squatting in the flap of
a tent below Snowdon.

You wear only your gaze, a sweater
that held on for your lifetime. Self-

warmed against sky and granite
you're kernel, courage.

I hold the last strands.

Wardian Case

Picture the biopic: Nathaniel enters
frock-coated.
London's a grey lithograph
and on this day again
fog ladles itself
all over his garden,
a stew of soot and suspect breath.

His aspidium is stifled; a coal skin
dumped on first-born tendrils
becomes the catalyst
(as dirt does).

Exotically challenged
he tinkers with the possible, sourly
like a summer-jaded boy

finds a moth pupa – heraldic
tough and blue black
as official leather. Seals it

in with a pinch of soil, seed. Observes.
(Observation is the 'helper'
in this tale, a mind for specimens
not the chaos of frippery wings.)

It's unofficial news that opens first,
the one that sneaked in:
a little ball of fern untwisting, unnatural circus
green as it scales the sides,
its unalloyed world.

Lives. Suspend this moment
in Nathaniel's eye, pressed-up to glass
an intake
as he sees his conquest, time-locked under glass
(and the monetary benefit).
Shoots from climates
too rare to handle, now holdable
as an iris by the white.

In little glass wombs they will come,
to arsenic parlours where he fancies
the whale-boned breath of women might beat
against its casing, moth-sucked
to such unreachable, wild, oxygen.

How to Raise a Salad in the 1600s

This is the house of glass, will admit what mortar or claggy brick
cannot, a speeding of things to meet your palate, for fruit in winter,
a fine tool of control. It will conjure pears in frost, and this green salad
in two brief hours. No devilry but the mere tweaking
of God's laws for the settled man who would choose the cut and colour
of his stomach's content, not, beast-like, wait in fallen dark
for the great ice to ease. Is not this enlightenment, to eat all seasons
at call! For the salad you must tell them a great fire make, drag
clooted horse dung they have gathered in the up and down year long,
burn also the moss that clothes a forest – send them with sacks
to uproot all day. This content they must burn to ashes, beat well
with staves, moisten with water of a dunghill, no matter how acrid
and burning to the eyes its stench. Thus make they a compost
black as a smouldered witch but wholesome as it heats. Its black
crumbles they must spread like indulgence over your seeds.
Keep moistened. Yours is the power of this odorous womb that soon
will crack forth shoots. The green looks well on blue porcelain.
Bones also, crushed, will speed the convenience.

Natural History

Starched to school file we pass 'Entrance'
the giant or extinct demand awe
and no back-chat in an over-arched hall
where the temperature drops like a 'shush'
for the chancel of mammoths
whose long-goneness dwarfs us.
Rather dioramas where lush murals box
brink-dramas between python and cute
not-looking, mammal. Always *in media res*
always on the edge of explicit
a throat savaged in our heads,
resin teeth that get away
through educational rock and moss.
It's kick-cum-disgrace of real kill,
more tease than slitting frogs,
but domestic – the make-do anneal
of glass eyes wedged in fur, passive
as we were when dads fixed dolls,
glue burning our nostrils while parts
fused, a dis-bodied face still attached
to a mute, blue, gaze that never slipped
or shifted. Each time the mend was harder.

But some days I'd rip a doll head or arm
for the thrill, to bring dad down
to the table with his brushes. To believe
he could make frayed joints meet
like two rivers. I'd circle as he set
in gritted patience.
Until one day he refused,
held up the head
with its worked-thin neck
pink strained
to dull yolk.
The silence then
of a blown egg.

The Museum of Ice

It opens at the dark time, a nerve that remembers
cold habits.
But we bought our tickets in May:
the queues build like sap, or how sap used to build
when there were timescapes
still to cross.

You may choose your pathways; we opt for colour
sensation ice as a multi-cake,
blue-mint, pink, a choco slab.
The visual makes it virtual for our kids
who have only Cold App
and no click back.

Blue ice is for glacial melt, Water-Melon's algae,
Brown is dirt from *deep time*,
which somehow lets us off – ancient smelting,
ash, Romanic lead dust.
They skip the worst
sunk in.

This museum's not an ethic, it's for re-enactment
like a muscle that wants
to clench in season. At the Hall of Everest
you may don a thermal suit
feel the knifing
white you out.

A ghost voice stuttery, susceptible to muffle
as the last walk on sludge
tells us this: there is such cold you can lose your mind in,
a euphoria that seizes at a certain height, a dazzle!
You must curl in the eardrum of now,
stay fixed.

And then they play the wind. And then they play the crush
and spark of someone crossing ice.
How there seems no end to it, just faith.
Then it does end. Ferried to the tepid canteen we slice
butter with a tiny plastic axe. Blunt
to why we longed.

The Fish Stall; They Peer At

fins in twisted ice   a giant seabass locked
mid–coil black   scales
like mushrooms   muscular

he's naming   bream mullet
mussel smells   sulphurous

tart   hormones of the ocean

chemistry sloshed   through gills

fishermen get addicted   itch
on land for it
                 she thinks   who'd throb
in this town of surrogate   ripples ice
creamed light the houses

                             storm
colours bleached   of storm's
bruise   hydrangea
shrimp

the fish–seller   striped apron
                             linen cap

it's all retail now, sexed-up crab with pickles

that's his boat in the harbour clacking
                 her ghost shanty

Diorama

Bell-jar, crinoline, chicanery

glass where stuffed fox or hawk, a fleshy coral
display the pose
of the pause before they could swoop

                                    bite,
                              swell
now décor. We are directed
to the taxidermist's drawer
                              his scalpel
                              blades
to scoop out an eye, his tongue-depressor.

A porn of cute, these jerkined rabbits
wired to their teacups, ape
the hour's pleasantry

which will occur within borders, coiffured,
contorted, boxwood
boxed
into the spectre of a wild tree.

Blindness is an atmosphere:
                              inside this case
                              an eyeless goddess, veined
                              a mask
                              a weasel
                              her stiff-dried teats.
The shape of air between them
thrums with dust.

Othering

Leaf through a forest
mulch of tea-coloured pages
in *The Book of Explorers*
whose faces bud from text, already leathery
under the whitish bloom of hats.
Most are twig within plus-fours, cling
to a skeletal insouciance.

The women get a page here:
'adventuresses'
they gaze with rigour, afraid of slack,
master the foreground, pillared
beside the smaller native
who've leaked curiously
into the frame, or been shuffled
in by command.
Temperate brown skirts expose
and encase
a cartooned startlement.

*

The trail back-tracks to outsets
litanies of what to take.
The ribbage not taken
a gorgeous vandalism
like dismantling the girders of a station, letting the glass
roof lift in one flight, no swaying hoops,
the walking cage that kept your stride
white and truncated, a fleshy ripple
under shadowy plaid
turning plum,
deep ivy,
bruise.

Isabella Bird in Canada

packed in her night and day:
her folding chair, her stretcher bed

to sleep, to dine, recline, articulate
as fathers did. And 'a light wrap for the evening'

as if to bring a smoking-hour gradation
to the darkness between sugar pine and redwood

where she could lurk among maps and measurements.
Her tents would be lace-work free but distant

and a little above the settlement of wigwams
observable a through a lens. She noted

'lank hair', an indolent look, but purchased bead
curios. Noted: 'these women are perfect savages'.

The Plant Hunter

Item: *there must be food in China*
                Joseph Hooker

He is a man of lists. It's like laying steps
across the river; you need to think in pebbles
when the jungle's losing you ten ways at once.
Tweeds for example, *camphor oil* and *String*.

China's the map on his desk: a lunar quilt,
massed creases that mean height and emptiness,
places where mules slide over, vertigo. Flowers.
Where there are flowers there are people

seeded to valleys, ledges, a yellow outcrop
of monks. Rice, eggs, fowl. Logic
is homespun and muscular, will get him
from meal to meal to the altitude for theft.

But first there is the moment when he transforms,
when he stands up at dawn above a forest
and sees the mountains gilded like a prize.
He'll possess the image before he breaks a stem.

To get that far you need to conserve your breath,
square up, scale down. *Jam* is essential
to civilise mush, and *whisky is antiseptic*
but nothing to dull the petals' unfingered blue.

Catalogue

Plant-presses, blotters, ink
a moustache worn curled
an aptitude for dangling off
a theory, hive-mind

of natives to act as porter, spirit
guide, lackey. Cigars,
adrenalin, an entitled extra metre
on most who live here

whose bushy rampant
speech you dismiss a jungle
of dialect yet may help to hack
through to the Latin

singular, *silene:campion*.
When you find her, tiny red mouth
in a crevice, froths back as you
pull, measure, dry her to a cipher.

Readings

'....well supplied with 42 advanced scientific instruments microscopes telescopes barometers thermometers a rain gauge quadrants and sextants a Leyden jar for storing static electricity a magnetic needle a galvanometer to measure electric currents and a pendulum.'

an instrument to compare degrees of blue in the colour of the sky

Find a high outcrop, not slippery,
you must stand clear of grikes or prejudice, avoid
lingering on your inner blue:

'blue is the colour of longing for the distances you never arrive in...blue is the light that got lost'
The difference in intensity between two
blues may be determined by the distance between
but this would be different for different eyes.

'the tiny sound of my shutter falling- that little trap-door catching light, opening and closing like the valves of the heart'
Between the sky and your eye
you must hold a standard – a circle of paper
segmented from white to black

'the Guide becomes...the very opposite of what it advertises an agent of blindness'
Between your eyes and the sky
find blue that meets a segment of the standard
Each blueness can be pulled out, pinned.

'(Doomree — Vegetation of table-land — Lieutenant Beadle — Birds — Hot springs of Soorujkoond — Plants near them — Shells in them — Cholera-tree — Olibanum — Palms, form of — Dunwah Pass — Trees, native and planted — Wild peacock — Poppy fields — Geography and geology of Behar and Central India — Toddy-palm — Ground, temperature of — Barroon — Temperature of plants — Lizard — Cross the Soane — Sand, ripple marks on — Kymore hills — Ground, temperature of — Limestone — Rotas fort and palace — Nitrate of lime — Change of climate — Lime stalagmites, enclosing leaves — Fall of Soane — Spiders, etc. — Scenery and natural history of upper Soane valley — Hardwickia binata — Bhel fruit — Dust-storm — Alligator — Catechu — Cochlospermum — Leaf-bellows — Scorpions — Tortoises — Florican — Limestone spheres — Coles — Tiger-hunt — Robbery.)'

Readings 2

Barometer

Each day of this journey is full of chasms
the mountains turn on and off between mists
Like blue light, to trigger the morning
he'll measure. Dew crazies

two thermometers he sinks into grass.
Later, a bellying shadow in a dust storm,
he anvils the barometer
against wind, notes *nothing could be observed*

disappointed. The day ends
with damage unlisted but an exact
inking-in of insects. He breaths
on glass tubes, wipes in moonlight.

Diorama

'Near Chanchee we passed an alligator, just killed by two men, a foul beast, about nine feet long, of the mugger kind. More absorbing than its natural history was the circumstance of its having swallowed a child.'

It is arranged to lie belly up, serrated jaws misaligned for effect. Flashback to the child playing in water while puppet-jaws loom from behind. We see the mother, eternally unseeing, washing her pans in the river. The brute is barely dead, its stomach swollen by the swallowed child. The mother stands beside it, wringing her hands, unable to tear her eyes from the dying creature, tenaciously clinging to life. Its slayers lean, battle-wearied on staves, from which the creature's blood still drips. We note the livid reds, the lurid jungle greens. At some distance a hovel, two gaunt cattle. The husband is sick. The lost child their future hope.

Note here, the *Butea frondosa* in flower, and a sublime sight indeed. Massed, the inflorescence suggests sheets of flame, and individually the flowers are notably beautiful, the bright orange-red petals enticing against brilliantly jet-black velvety calyx. The nest of the *Megachile* (leaf-cutter bee) was everywhere on the cliffs, with Mayflies, Caddis-worms, spiders.

Cranogwen

Sewing

Rows of women in this long room
repeating ourselves over and over
in the same motion, tacking, grey
boats, moored to our needles.
Wrists dip, rise, dip. No visible land.

What to think of as I patch? Home
will not bleat out of fog, thoughts of dawn
mussel-coloured above Cranog
could unravel me. The day sinks to its knees
in the end, but nothing changes pitch.

My cloth is baize, toneless, doesn't ripple
through the spectrum as sea does
gun-whale to gull's egg, crested, pinked.
The brown feather is always female.
Which is why I downed cloth, found my stride

back to where father's jerry mooned.
He'd packed my mind
with latitude: I leant like a man
one elbow on the sea-chest.
Freedom, I told him, is knowing how to steer.

Still he could not account for a woman
so stray-tuned, yet gave me the ship's wheel,
compass, a pat of course.
But in this village we all lean
into the sea's derangements,

you will slip under
without a grip on mathematics.
I bit wind for a voice,
rouged my cheeks in Noon Sun
peered across the sextant's crinoline,

set the needle beyond my length.

Llangrannog

is all about verticals: not straight
but bulge-edged and muscley
from meeting the waves' punch-bag.

Cliff as pours of lava
heaped in towers like black laundry
upsetting the rule of square
sea's washing
takes the air away
always in the face
of houses pegged out
on crevices, the wrinkled gorse.

Salt cakes church slates, porches
are chipped palladian, like relics
thrown inland with herring bones and blue
knots of seaweed, twine, Perspex.

More ship than stability
more crab-claw than root
living with the roof off –
who wouldn't sharpen
their calculations in this wind?
Tug the great sea-press in
on a line of brass instruments?

How to Raise a Himalayan Blue

Here, a sub-genre among the books of growth and weeding
for a thin but persistent market: the blue-addicted.
and not just any blue, but poppy blueness.

Supra-lit on seed packets
achingly in your face,
their petals glow
an improbable
Arctic
fresco
thrush-egg
crystal
meth, planet, iris
of an old seadog, will flood
your veins with the hope of it

which is slight
and not at one with the climate

whose tepid flow won't wake them.
There is a trick:
you catch seed young
fool them with bogus winter.

What do the seeds believe
as they cleave to soaked kitchen paper
in a freezer, among packets
of pork-loin and breast
with their codes for longevity?

Eye-pits, stuffed
with the blue silk
of their memory

will do what seeds do.
To the brief
stare of their flowers, you are a void
that blocks the sun, a little less time.

Log

A day sail from home berth.
1500 dropped main near Pye End buoy.
Ran n under jib.
Wind sw/23
1620 near Guard buoy, furled up jib,
continued under power.

Locked out. Fetched cliff Ft by under-power 2000rpm.
Unfurled genoa. Stopped engine. Beam reach.
Started autohelm. 3ks. Fetched stonebks by. Course change.
Haze. Haze invisible. Fetched Medusa by.
Turned back.

Cork Sand By.
Gristle By.
Pye End By.
Medusa By.
Haze.

A day sail from home berth.
Fetched Stone banks by.
3 cables from Medusa. Unfurled Genny.
Stopped engine.
Fetched Stone banks by. Furled Genny.
H 27. Medusa
Turned back. Haze
invisible.

Minik

At his funeral, my father turned invisible: he
who'd been eyed by thousands – his caribou a hint
at the sharp white fear they were missing, stink of a kill.
They hid his corpse under furs. Only later did I learn
it was trickery, a log in wolf's clothing. The curators bowed
oiled heads as the dead wood passed them, theatric
down a box-lined avenue. They squeezed my hand.

In fact, he was having the time of his death!
Skinned, scoured, bleached, numbered, his bones polished
for the cabinet. Which I later found. And when the stone
blocking my breath lifted for a moment, I silently asked
my father how he would rearrange the view?
What would be the engine? Would he place at its heart
that Arctic seal, yellow light steaming from its dive?

Annunciation

The angel was called Hermes, was there and then he wasn't.
She'd been painting her nails with blue varnish
and had to keep her hands out like spokes
as it all sank in, although she wanted to run for caffeine.

It arrived on a light-shaft from an unknown power source
instant delivery, but no options for feedback on the packaging
which was see-through but toughened. She squinted
at the godlet in his one-man galaxy shaped like a tear.

The instructions said to place in water and watch it grow:
she remembered a story about a baby crocodile in a bath
who went overnight from cute lizardy wriggle to very large
and toothy. She kept a close eye on the holy milk-teeth

but they never became serious. In fact he ate so little
she googled male eating disorder: there was nothing
on divinity. He stayed thin and mealy coloured
grew his hair long but only tried a man-bun for a month

was into vinyl, upset her by joining a marginal cult.
She wondered if there was a design fault,
Hermes had called the blueprint 'inviolable' as if it had a poor surface
like old prit-stick, for viols and violets. Or it could be akin

to some hard-set word you might miss in the small print
of a loan agreement. Was it meant to be reassuring?
There were no real guidelines and no God the Father manifested
with his feet on the ground, kicking a ball about.

She'd applied for maintenance by phone but got put on hold
then diverted to a liminal zone where they played the soundtrack
to Pulp Fiction between ads for breast enhancement
and smart phone upgrades. It was the age of incarnate lifestyle.

When they finally answered she was told he could not be returned
and they were sorry he didn't mirror the original but these days
so much gets hacked into. They tried to match product
to expectation, but these days data is so rapid, decays in a flash.

Melanin

This suitcase is not new: all year it's malingered
in the loft-dark, growing slack. The zip snags
on its tracks, chews in. Work it, rung
by rung, until the lid flips back
on silk's carnage, still trying to take the weight:
creases collapsed in soft, incremental, landslides.

Turn it to sift out sand, pill-packet, a bee
now powder, a feather, blue-black with a seam like ice
as seen from space. Melanin's a creosote for wings,
for the long fly, keeps out, holds in.

This suitcase might be for birds or for bricks,
for winged shoes, or black clothes at a funeral
for selves like soft-tissue: pack –
downable at first, but will leak though
the held-in air. This suitcase restores
the dent of flight in mist,
a rosta of starlings, a pioneer
dressed in numbers, scavengers
of outline, archivists of blue.

What the Burglar Took

That night it was nothing.
Cinematic, he'd slid
under the kitchen window,
swerved an old veined saucer,
rocked the vintage cactus,
slippered his way across tiles
on a moulting rug
that still smelt of your last dog
and made you wheeze.

After that threshold no sign,
yet you felt him in every omission
the carriage clock that paced him
but never chimed, silverfish
partying by moonlight who'd fled
into covens of dust, slivers
of streetlamp that laid a grid
from back to front room
where shadows failed to creak.

His exit, another window,
half open in the study.
The room was rigid with night,
The Great Bear
encrypted in the cushions.
You touched frost on the inside,
took to spying on your house,
heard whispers in the heating kettle
Morse in the water-pipes.

Notes & Acknowledgements

'Consolidant' is inspired by an artwork by the Danish artist and film maker Wilmhelm Freddie (1909–1995).

'Wardian Case' recalls the accidental discovery by doctor and botanist Nathaniel Bagshaw Ward (1791–1868) of the preservative properties of sealed glass. He invented a glass case for transporting, or growing, plants, known as the 'Wardian Case'.

'Isabella Bird in Canada' is based on extracts from a collection of letters by the explorer Isabella Bird (1831-1904) See Isabella Bird *A Lady's Life in the Rocky Mountains* (Renaissance Classics 2012).

'Readings' & 'Readings 2' are inspired by the Himalayan journals of the plant hunter Joseph Hooker. I adapt extracts from the journals in a collage-like fashion, to give a sense of the style and reading experience. See J.D. Hooker *Himalayan Journals Complete* (General Books LLC 2010). The small text above the stanzas in 'Readings' are 'found' quotes on the topic of blue.

'Minik' was inspired by the story of an Inuit man named Minik Wallace who was brought to New York's Museum of Natural History with his father and four others by the explorer Robert Peary in 1897. Minik's father died of disease, and a false burial was staged for Minik. His father was actually preserved as a specimen, on display in the museum, which Minik eventually came upon.

Thank you to Matthew Francis for his critiques of many of these poems during a PhD at Aberystwyth University, to Philip Fried, for publishing some of these poems in *The Manhattan Review*. Thanks likewise to Nia Davis, former editor of *Poetry Wales* who has also published poems from the collection, as too the editors of *The Lampeter Review*, Patricia McCarthy, editor of *Agenda*, and John Lavin, editor of *The Lonely Crowd*. Thanks to Mario Petrucci for awarding Highly Commended to the poem 'Isinglass' in the Cinnamon Press Single Poem Competition 2014, and to Jean Atkins for awarding first prize to the poem 'The Plant Hunter' in the Cinnamon Press Single Poem Competition 2015. Thanks to Billy Collins for long-listing 'Minutiae' in the 2019 Fish Poetry Prize. Gratitude to the trustees of the Hawthornden Fellowships, for awarding me a writing retreat at Hawthornden Castle (2017). Thanks to Jacob Polley, Maura Dooley, Jean Sprackland and Gillian Clarke for invaluable feedback at various workshops. Also deepest thanks to my Welsh literary friends who have offered advice, cups of coffee or kind words. In particular Samantha Wynne-Rhydderch, whose support and poetic judgement have always been invaluable. Enormous thanks to the Seren team and my wonderful editor, Amy Wack.

Thanks to Literature Wales for the award of a 2018 Literature Wales Writer's Bursary supported by the National Lottery through Arts Council of Wales.